Running WILD
The Untold Story of America's Mustangs

Explore the Heritage, Struggles, and Conservation Efforts to Save these Iconic Wild Horses from Losing Their Freedom

JENNIFER GLASSMAN

© Copyright Jennifer Glassman - 2025 - All rights reserved.

The content within this book may not be reproduced, duplicated or transmitted without direct written permission from the author or the publisher.

Under no circumstances will any blame or legal responsibility be held against the publisher, or author, for any damages, reparation, or monetary loss due to the information contained within this book. Either directly or indirectly. You are responsible for your own choices, actions, and results.

Legal Notice:

This book is copyright protected. This book is only for personal use. You cannot amend, distribute, sell, use, quote or paraphrase any part, of the content within this book, without the consent of the author or publisher.

Disclaimer Notice:

Please note the information contained within this document is for educational and entertainment purposes only. All effort has been expended to present accurate, up-to-date, and reliable, complete information. No warranties of any kind are declared or implied. Readers acknowledge that the author is not engaging in the rendering of legal, financial, medical or professional advice. The content within this book has been derived from various sources. Please consult a licensed professional before attempting any techniques outlined in this book.

By reading this document, the reader agrees that under no circumstances is the author responsible for any losses, direct or indirect, which are incurred as a result of the use of the information contained within this document, including, but not limited to, — errors, omissions, or inaccuracies.

Table of Contents

Chapter 1: Origins of the American Mustang 15

Chapter 2: The Mustang's Role in American History 23

Chapter 3: Modern Challenges Facing Mustangs 31

Chapter 4: Conservation and Advocacy Efforts 39

Chapter 5: A Day in the Life on the Sanctuary 49

Chapter 6: Visual Storytelling through Photography 57

Chapter 7: The Future of the American Mustang 63

Chapter 8: Mustang Advocacy and Community Engagement 67

Conclusion 75

About the Author 79

References 82

"The wind of heaven is that which blows between a horse's ears."
– Arabian Proverb

A band of Mustangs gallops across the open plains in the cool dawn light of the American West. Their manes ripple in the wind, and their hooves thunder against the earth. Dust rises in clouds behind them. The air is alive with the sound of their freedom, and the world feels timeless for a moment. These wild horses, symbols of strength and independence, have roamed these lands for centuries.

But what IS a Mustang? Simply, it's a horse born in the "American wild." By definition, a horse is considered a Mustang if it is born a free-roaming horse of the Western United States, mainly descended from horses brought to the Americas by Spanish explorers in the 16th century. Mustangs are descendants of domesticated horses that escaped or were released and have adapted to survive in the wild. Over generations, they have become a distinct population of feral horses known for their resilience, toughness, and ability to thrive in harsh environments. The term "Mustang" itself comes from the Spanish word "mesteño," meaning "stray" or "wild."

Did you know horses originally lived in North America thousands of years ago, long before the Mustangs? This fact is one of the many things that led me to this book. As a Mustang owner, lover, and supporter, I wanted to understand their past – not simply string together things I saw on Facebook.

Mustangs were native species roaming the land until they went extinct around 10,000 years ago, likely due to climate change and human activity. The 16th century was when Spanish explorers brought horses back to the continent. These domesticated horses eventually escaped or were set free, adapting to the wild and becoming what we now know as Mustangs. So, while Mustangs are often seen as wild, they're actually feral descendants of those European horses, not related to the ancient horses that once lived here long before humans.

Mustangs are often seen as symbols of the American frontier and represent freedom, independence, and the untamed spirit of the wilderness. They are not a specific breed but rather a population with mixed ancestry, influenced by various horse breeds over time.

The future of Mustangs is at risk as they are systematically rounded up and removed from their natural habitats. Many of these iconic animals end up in holding facilities funded by taxpayer dollars, where they are often forgotten. Without immediate action, the American Mustang, a powerful symbol of freedom, may soon disappear from the landscape.

This book offers an in-depth exploration of the American Mustang, tracing its rich history, cultural significance, and current challenges. The author aims to raise awareness through personal experiences and compelling photography of Mustangs in the wild and captivity. It is

hoped that readers will feel inspired to reach out to their Senators and Congressmen to advocate for the end of these cruel roundups and support the development of more sustainable and humane solutions for Mustang population management.

The Mustangs are more than just horses; they are living icons of freedom and resilience. Their beauty captivates us, but their plight demands our attention.

Mustangs have played a vital role in American history. Once brought over by Spanish explorers, they adapted to the wild and became part of the landscape. They represent the spirit of the West, embodying a sense of possibility and adventure. Ecologically, they contribute to the biodiversity of the regions they inhabit. Culturally, they have inspired countless stories, artworks, and songs. They are a testament to nature's tenacity and grace.

My connection to these magnificent creatures runs deep. As a Mustang photographer, I have spent countless hours capturing their beauty through my lens. Each photograph tells a story. Each moment in their presence renews my commitment to their cause. My work goes beyond images. I advocate tirelessly for their protection and provide sanctuary to those who have lost their freedom. This book is a part of that effort, a way to raise awareness and inspire action.

The book unfolds in several parts. We begin with the historical context, tracing the Mustangs' journey from their origins to their iconic status in American culture. Next, we delve into the challenges they face today, from habitat loss to legal battles. We also explore the efforts of conservationists and advocates working to protect them. Throughout, personal stories and anecdotes bring the narrative to life, offering a glimpse into the emotional bond between humans and these wild horses.

The threats facing Mustangs are urgent and real. Their habitats are shrinking due to development and land-use changes, leaving them vulnerable to horrific and cruel round-ups with helicopters and splitting up family bands and ultimately - captivity. The situation is dire, but not hopeless. Immediate action is needed to ensure their survival.

I invite you to engage with this cause. Whether through advocacy, education, or direct action, every effort counts. By learning about the Mustangs and their struggles, you become part of their story. Together, we can make a difference.

This book is more than just facts and figures. It's is what started my emotional journey – and so many other people that I've met along the way…that will touch your heart. Through the stories of individual Mustangs, those who fight for them, and those who are healed by

them, you will discover the transformative power of these horses. They teach us about resilience, hope, and the importance of standing up for what we cherish.

As you turn these pages, I leave you with a question: What will the future hold for the American Mustang? In a world that often prioritizes progress over preservation, how will we choose to protect these symbols of freedom? The answers lie in our actions and our willingness to fight for the wild spirit that the Mustangs embody.

Chapter 1:
Origins of the American Mustang

"A man on a horse is spiritually as well as physically bigger than a man on foot."
– John Steinbeck

The saga of the American Mustang begins long before their gallop through the Western plains etched them into the mythos of freedom and wildness. It is a story steeped in transformation and adaptation, tracing back to the late 15th century—a pivotal era marked by exploration, conquest, and change. In these pages, we unravel the intricate narrative of how horses arrived in the Americas, profoundly altering landscapes and societies. Their introduction not only heralded a new epoch for the land but also deeply intertwined with the lives of the indigenous peoples who had long thrived here, creating a bond that reshaped the continent's destiny.

As the 15th century drew to a close, the world teetered on the edge of profound change. Driven by ambition, curiosity, and the lure of uncharted wealth, European explorers launched expeditions that bridged worlds. Among them was Christopher Columbus, whose 1493 voyage to the Caribbean marked a seminal moment in the history of the Americas. Aboard this journey were the first horses introduced to the New World, a contingent of creatures whose arrival would set the stage for profound ecological and cultural shifts.

For indigenous peoples, the sight of these majestic animals—powerful, swift, and otherworldly—must have evoked awe and bewilderment. To societies that had never before encountered horses, these animals seemed like beings from myth. Yet, as awe gave way

to understanding, the potential of these animals became evident. Horses revolutionized indigenous hunting techniques, making the pursuit of game faster and more efficient. Warfare also transformed, as the speed and agility of mounted warriors tipped the scales of intertribal conflicts, altering the balance of power. Horses became economic assets, linking previously isolated communities through extended trade routes and fostering the exchange of goods, ideas, and culture.

Initially confined to coastal settlements in the Caribbean, horses quickly spread inland as Spanish explorers and settlers ventured into the Americas. However, this expansion was not without hurdles. North and South America's diverse climates—from arid deserts to dense rainforests—posed unique challenges. Horses, accustomed to Europe's temperate regions, had to adapt to new predators, unfamiliar diseases, and fierce competition for food and water. Over time, these challenges forged a hardy breed capable of thriving in the untamed wilderness. It was during these formative years that the seeds of the Mustang's legendary resilience were sown, as these animals evolved into symbols of survival and strength.

The early 16th century ushered in an era of Spanish conquests, profoundly shaping the destiny of the Mustang. Explorers such as Hernán Cortés recognized the strategic value of horses, whose strength, speed, and sheer presence struck fear into opponents and symbolized dominion. In 1519, Cortés's expedition to Mexico introduced horses to the mainland, where they played pivotal roles in the Spanish campaign to subdue the Aztec Empire. Horses were not merely tools of war; they were the lifeblood of Spanish expeditions, enabling the conquest and colonization of vast territories.

Spain's imperial ambitions extended beyond conquest to settlement. The establishment of missions and ranches throughout the Americas created centers for breeding and disseminating horses. Spanish monks and settlers meticulously bred horses suited to the demands of this new world, blending breeds like the Andalusian—known for its grace—and the Barb, revered for its endurance. This genetic melding laid the foundation for the Mustang's unique characteristics: strength, agility, and resilience.

Yet, human oversight only went so far. As Spanish ranches expanded, the occasional escape or abandonment of horses led to the formation of free-roaming herds. Over time, these escaped horses embraced their freedom, carving out a life in the wild. This transition from domesticated laborer to untamed wanderer was neither immediate nor easy, but it marked the genesis of the Mustang's identity. These horses adapted to the vast North American plains, forming herds, navigating harsh conditions, and embracing the untamed spirit of the land.

The evolution of the Mustang into a wild, free-roaming horse is a testament to adaptability. Over generations, Mustangs developed enhanced endurance, speed, and agility, traits that became essential for survival in the vast, often unforgiving landscapes of North America. They learned to traverse immense distances in search of food and water, their muscular bodies growing lean and efficient. Their powerful lungs and sturdy legs allowed them to gallop tirelessly across open plains.

Dietary habits also adapted to the harsh realities of their environment. Mustangs became opportunistic grazers, capable of subsisting on a variety of grasses, shrubs, and vegetation. Whether enduring the tough, fibrous grasses of the Great Plains or the sparse vegetation of desert regions, their flexibility allowed them to thrive in a multitude of habitats.

Ecologically, Mustangs played a critical role in maintaining balance. Despite modern debates on their environmental impact, their grazing habits historically prevented certain plant species from dominating, promoting biodiversity. Their interactions with native fauna were equally complex; as they competed with other herbivores for resources, they also became integral to the food chain, serving as prey for predators like wolves and mountain lions.

Genetic diversity further enhanced their adaptability. Throughout history, feral Mustangs interbred with horses brought by later settlers, enriching their gene pool. A poignant example is the Dust Bowl era of the 1930s, when desperate farmers released their horses into the wild due to economic hardship. These horses, integrated into existing Mustang herds, added genetic resilience and broadened their population's diversity.

The relationship between Mustangs and Native American tribes stands as one of the most profound cultural bonds in history. For many tribes, horses were more than just animals—they were partners in survival, revered symbols of strength, freedom, and spiritual connection. Mustangs transformed indigenous societies, enabling tribes to hunt more effectively, expand their territories, and build economies rooted in mobility.

The Comanche, often dubbed the "Lords of the Plains," epitomized the transformative impact of Mustangs. Renowned for their unparalleled horsemanship, the Comanche built a culture around these horses, using them for hunting, warfare, and trade. Similarly, the Navajo wove Mustangs into their spiritual and practical lives, viewing them as symbols of resilience and integrating them into agricultural practices and folklore.

As European settlers pushed westward, Mustangs became indispensable. Their strength, endurance, and adaptability made them valuable assets for agriculture, transportation, and exploration. Mustangs pulled plows, hauled goods, and served as mounts for pioneers navigating rugged terrains. In many ways, they were partners in the settlers' quest to tame the wilderness.

However, the relationship between settlers and Mustangs was not without tension. As Mustang populations grew, conflicts arose over grazing land and water. Many settlers viewed wild horses as competitors to their livestock and sought to control or eradicate herds. These tensions often culminated in round-ups, culls, and legal battles—conflicts that continue to shape debates about the Mustang's place in modern America.

Popular culture has romanticized Mustangs as wild creatures, untethered from human influence. However, the reality is more nuanced. Mustangs are feral horses, descendants of those introduced by the Spanish and later settlers. Their genetic makeup reflects a mosaic of breeds, from Andalusians to Barbs and beyond, shaped by centuries of adaptation.

This blend of myth and fact underscores the Mustang's enduring appeal. They are not relics of a distant past but living symbols of resilience, embodying the intersection of human history and natural evolution. By understanding their true origins, we honor the depth and complexity of their story—a story that mirrors the spirit of adaptation and survival that defines the American West.

The story of the American Mustang is one of transformation and resilience. From their arrival as domesticated animals to their evolution into symbols of freedom, Mustangs have become an integral part of the American narrative. They embody the spirit of the land, a living testament to the power of adaptability and survival. As we continue to grapple with their future, the Mustang reminds us of our shared history and the enduring bond between humans, animals, and the untamed wilderness.

Chapter 2:
The Mustang's Role in American History

"There is something about the outside of a horse that is good for the inside of a man."
– Winston Churchill

Imagine the sprawling expanse of the American frontier, a landscape where the horizon extends endlessly, meeting a sky that knows no bounds. In this vast, untamed wilderness, the Mustang emerges as a pivotal figure. More than a wild animal, it became a symbol of resilience and freedom, an enduring partner to the settlers who ventured west in pursuit of new opportunities. The Mustang, with its unmatched endurance, adaptability, and spirit, played an instrumental role in the expansion of the American frontier, a journey that would shape the nation's history and identity. To settlers, Mustangs were not just beasts of burden—they were indispensable companions in the colossal task of building a nation.

As pioneers and settlers heeded the call of Manifest Destiny, the 19th century saw thousands of people traverse unforgiving terrains in search of land, prosperity, and freedom. The westward expansion was a grueling endeavor, requiring immense resilience, and for this monumental task, the Mustang proved indispensable. Pioneers depended on these horses to transport their possessions, pulling heavy wagons over rugged trails, barren deserts, and snow-laden mountain passes. The harsh conditions of the frontier demanded horses that could endure extreme temperatures, navigate treacherous paths, and survive on meager forage—and Mustangs were uniquely suited to meet these challenges.

Their surefootedness, remarkable stamina, and ability to subsist on sparse vegetation made Mustangs the perfect partner for the arduous journey west. These horses were not only survivors but also enablers of human survival, ensuring that settlers reached their

destinations despite the daunting obstacles in their path. Without the Mustang, the vast migration to the western territories might have been slower and fraught with even greater hardships. For many settlers, the Mustang was more than just a tool—it was a lifeline.

In addition to their role in transportation, Mustangs significantly influenced the economic development of the frontier. While imported horses were costly and often ill-suited for the demands of frontier life, Mustangs provided a practical and affordable alternative. Their low maintenance needs, ability to thrive in the wild, and widespread availability made them accessible to even the poorest settlers. As a result, Mustangs helped facilitate commerce, enabling settlers to establish trade routes across the frontier.

Trails that had once been deemed impassable transformed into bustling arteries of commerce, connecting remote settlements to emerging markets. Mustangs carried goods, supplies, and people, serving as the backbone of a developing economy. Their resilience made it possible to move resources across vast distances, and their strength allowed settlers to cultivate new lands, fostering agricultural growth. In many ways, Mustangs were both the vehicle and the engine of economic progress, transforming isolated outposts into thriving communities.

As Mustangs roamed freely across the plains, their impact extended beyond human society, shaping the ecosystems they inhabited. Their grazing habits helped maintain plant diversity in many areas, preventing certain species from overgrowing and creating opportunities for other flora to thrive. However, their introduction to the Americas also brought competition. Mustangs competed with native herbivores, such as elk and deer, for food and water, sometimes straining already limited resources in arid regions. In some cases, this competition led to habitat depletion, altering the composition of local ecosystems.

Despite these challenges, Mustangs became a key part of the ecological balance. Their presence influenced predator-prey dynamics, as they became a food source for predators such as wolves and mountain lions. In turn, Mustangs carved out a unique role within the natural tapestry of the West, becoming a fixture of its ecological and cultural identity.

The rapid expansion of human settlements brought inevitable conflicts between settlers and Mustang herds. As land was claimed for agriculture, settlers often viewed Mustangs as competitors for valuable grazing land. This perception led to efforts to control Mustang populations, which ranged from organized round-ups to the hunting of herds. These measures, while intended to protect resources, often threatened the survival of Mustangs and diminished their numbers.

The tension between human expansion and the preservation of wild horses underscored a broader theme: the challenge of balancing economic development with environmental stewardship. This conflict continues to resonate in modern conservation debates, reflecting the enduring struggle to coexist with nature in a rapidly changing world.

Beyond their practical contributions, Mustangs became enduring symbols of the American frontier spirit. To settlers and cowboys, they represented freedom, resilience, and the untamed beauty of the West. The Mustang's ability to thrive in harsh conditions mirrored the settlers' own determination and grit. This shared struggle fostered a deep bond between human and horse, one that transcended mere utility.

In folklore and popular imagination, the Mustang took on a near-mythical status. Stories of wild Mustangs galloping across the open plains, untamed and unconquerable, captured the public's imagination. These tales celebrated the Mustang as an emblem of the untamed wilderness and the freedom it represented, reinforcing its place as an iconic figure in the narrative of the American West.

Among the many figures shaped by the Mustang, the cowboy stands out as perhaps the most iconic. For cowboys, Mustangs were more than just mounts; they were trusted partners in a demanding way of life. Cowboys relied on Mustangs for herding cattle, traversing rocky terrains, and enduring the long, grueling days of ranch work. The Mustang's agility and intelligence made it ideally suited for the challenges of cowboy life, while its resilience allowed it to thrive in the rugged conditions of the West.

Training Mustangs required patience, skill, and an intimate understanding of horse behavior. Cowboys developed techniques to tame these wild horses, transforming them into dependable work partners. This process, rooted in mutual trust and respect, created a unique bond between cowboy and horse. Over time, this partnership became a defining feature of cowboy culture, immortalized in songs, stories, and rodeos.

Mustangs also played a crucial role in American military history, particularly during the Indian Wars of the late 19th century. Their endurance, surefootedness, and ability to survive in harsh conditions made them invaluable to cavalry units operating in the challenging landscapes of the West. Mustangs carried soldiers across deserts, mountains, and plains, providing mobility and tactical advantages in battles.

Their contributions extended into the 20th century, particularly during World War I. While mechanization was beginning to transform warfare, Mustangs remained essential as pack animals, transporting supplies and equipment across rugged European terrains. Their resilience under fire and ability to navigate difficult landscapes earned them the respect and admiration of soldiers, cementing their legacy as invaluable military assets.

Today, the story of the Mustang is one of survival in the face of ongoing challenges. As human populations expand and land use changes, the habitats that Mustangs depend on continue to shrink. Debates over their impact on grazing lands and ecosystems have led to controversial population control measures, including round-ups and relocations. Advocacy groups dedicated to preserving Mustang herds have emerged, emphasizing their cultural and ecological significance.

Conservation efforts often draw on the Mustang's symbolic power, highlighting its role as a living testament to the American frontier spirit. These initiatives aim not only to protect Mustangs but also to preserve the landscapes they inhabit, ensuring that future generations can witness the beauty of these iconic animals in the wild.

In many ways, the Mustang's journey mirrors the broader American narrative—a story of survival, adaptation, and the pursuit of freedom. These horses, once introduced to the Americas as tools of colonization, have transformed into symbols of independence and resilience. Their presence in art, literature, and folklore reflects the deep cultural significance they hold, serving as reminders of the untamed wilderness that once defined the nation.

As we reflect on the role of Mustangs in the westward expansion and beyond, we are reminded of the enduring bond between humans and the natural world. The Mustang's legacy is not just one of survival but of partnership, resilience, and mutual respect. In honoring this legacy, we preserve a vital part of our shared history and ensure that the spirit of the Mustang continues to inspire for generations to come.

Chapter 3:
Modern Challenges Facing Mustangs

*"A horse is the projection of people's dreams about themselves—strong, powerful, beautiful—
and it has the capability of giving us escape from our mundane existence."*
– Pam Brown

Picture a Mustang, its sleek form silhouetted against the setting sun, standing atop a ridge that once seemed boundless. Today, however, that horizon is encroached upon by the relentless march of urbanization. As cities expand and suburbs sprawl, the open lands that Mustangs call home are disappearing, forcing these iconic creatures into ever-narrowing corridors. The encroachment of human development into Mustang territories not only diminishes their freedom but also threatens their existence, intensifying conflicts between humans and wildlife. To understand the plight of the Mustangs, one must consider the shrinking spaces they inhabit and the challenges these changes pose for their survival.

The relentless advance of urban sprawl has profound implications for Mustang habitats. Open grazing lands, once vast and inviting, are now being replaced by subdivisions, shopping centers, and industrial developments. As humans reshape the landscape to meet their needs, the areas where Mustangs once roamed freely are becoming fragmented. This fragmentation severely limits the Mustangs' ability to access vital resources such as water, food, and shelter. Over time, these isolated patches of habitat can no longer support sustainable populations, creating a cascade of challenges that threaten the survival of these free-roaming horses.

Infrastructure development plays a significant role in this fragmentation. Highways and railroads crisscross formerly open landscapes, acting as physical barriers that confine Mustangs to smaller areas. These man-made divides not only restrict the horses' movement but also pose direct dangers. Collisions between vehicles and Mustangs are an increasingly tragic reality, with devastating consequences for both the animals and humans involved. Moreover, the expansion of agricultural lands further exacerbates the problem, as fields and pastures compete with natural ecosystems, reducing the resources available to Mustangs and other wildlife.

As Mustang habitats shrink, the delicate balance of ecosystems is disrupted. Mustangs play a vital role in their environments, from grazing patterns that promote vegetation growth to aiding in seed dispersal. Their presence enhances biodiversity by supporting a variety of plant and animal species. However, as their habitats become smaller and more fragmented, this biodiversity diminishes, weakening the resilience of entire ecosystems.

The ecological implications of reduced Mustang populations extend beyond the horses themselves. Mustangs contribute to ecosystem services such as soil enrichment and water distribution, which benefit other species and the environment as a whole. Their absence creates gaps in these processes, leading to imbalances that affect everything from plant life to predator-prey relationships. This loss of ecological stability not only impacts the natural world but also affects humans by reducing the services that healthy ecosystems provide, such as water filtration and carbon storage.

To mitigate the effects of urbanization and habitat fragmentation, conservationists have proposed several strategies. Wildlife corridors are a promising solution, connecting isolated habitats and allowing Mustangs to move freely across the landscape. These corridors help maintain genetic diversity, support herd health, and reduce the risk of inbreeding. Land conservation initiatives also play a crucial role. By preserving critical areas of open land, these efforts provide Mustangs with the space they need to thrive while safeguarding biodiversity.

Successful conservation requires collaboration among government agencies, conservation organizations, local communities, and private landowners. Programs that incentivize land stewardship and habitat restoration can encourage individuals and organizations to participate in protecting Mustang habitats. Public awareness campaigns, too, are essential, fostering a sense of shared responsibility for preserving these iconic animals and the ecosystems they inhabit.

One of the most significant milestones in Mustang conservation was the passage of the Wild Free-Roaming Horses and Burros Act of 1971. Signed into law by President Richard Nixon, the act granted federal protection to Mustangs and recognized them as "living symbols of the historic and pioneer spirit of the West." This landmark legislation aimed to preserve the freedom of Mustangs on public lands, ensuring their place in the American landscape. However, in the decades since its enactment, the act has faced numerous challenges and amendments that have complicated its implementation.

The Public Rangelands Improvement Act of 1978, for example, introduced requirements for herd management and population counts. While intended to improve rangeland conditions, these measures also paved the way for more stringent population control efforts. Over time, conflicts between conservation goals and land use priorities have led to legal battles over the interpretation and enforcement of Mustang protections. Advocacy groups frequently challenge federal agencies in court, arguing that current policies fail to uphold the original spirit of the 1971 Act.

Central to these debates is the role of the Bureau of Land Management (BLM), the federal agency tasked with managing Mustang populations on public lands. The BLM employs strategies such as horrific, life-ending round-ups, fertility control, and adoption programs to maintain what it deems as appropriate management levels. However, these methods are controversial. Critics argue that round-ups are inhumane and that fertility control measures require greater oversight. Additionally, the conditions in holding facilities for captured Mustangs have been the subject of earned scrutiny, with real concerns about overcrowding and the overall care and welfare of the horses.

Overpopulation poses a significant challenge to Mustang conservation. As herds grow, they can exceed the carrying capacity of their habitats, leading to overgrazing and land degradation. In overpopulated areas, Mustangs may strip the land of vegetation faster than it can recover, leaving barren patches that struggle to support life. This not only impacts the Mustangs but also threatens other species that share the ecosystem.

Efforts to address overpopulation include fertility control measures, such as contraceptive darts, which aim to reduce reproduction rates in a humane and non-lethal manner. Adoption programs also provide an outlet for managing excess horses by placing them in private care. However, these programs face their own challenges, including limited capacity and the need for thorough screening to

ensure that adopted horses receive proper care. Often adopted Mustangs will end up at auction, and ultimately be shipped across our Nation's borders to be slaughtered for their meat.

The image of helicopters herding Mustangs into corrals has become synonymous with the controversial practice of round-ups. While round-ups are intended to control population numbers and relocate horses for adoption, they are deeply polarizing. Critics argue that the stress and injury caused by round-ups outweigh their benefits. The use of helicopters can panic the horses, leading to

injuries and even fatalities. Additionally, separating herds during round-ups disrupts familial and social structures, breaking bonds between mares, foals, and stallions.

Alternative methods, such as passive trapping, offer more humane approaches. These techniques involve luring Mustangs into enclosures using food and water, reducing the chaos and stress associated with helicopter round-ups. Advances in technology, such as drones and remote monitoring, also present opportunities to manage Mustang populations with minimal disruption to their natural behaviors.

As if urbanization and overpopulation were not enough, climate change adds another layer of complexity to Mustang conservation. Rising temperatures and shifting weather patterns are altering the landscapes where Mustangs live. Droughts are reducing water availability, while extreme weather events like storms and heatwaves challenge the horses' resilience. These changes force Mustangs to adapt, often by migrating to new areas in search of resources, which can lead to conflicts with humans and other wildlife.

Habitat restoration projects can help mitigate some of the impacts of climate change. By improving water management and planting climate-resilient vegetation, conservationists can create more sustainable habitats for Mustangs. Research into adaptive strategies is also essential, enabling Mustangs to cope with the new realities of their environment.

The future of Mustang conservation lies in finding a balance between human needs and the preservation of wild spaces. Collaborative approaches that bring together federal agencies, conservationists, ranchers, and local communities offer the best chance for success. By prioritizing habitat preservation, promoting sustainable management practices, and fostering public awareness, we can ensure that Mustangs continue to roam freely across the American landscape.

The Mustang's journey from a symbol of untamed wilderness to a species fighting for survival underscores the broader challenges of coexistence in a rapidly changing world. Preserving their legacy requires commitment, innovation, and a shared vision for the future—a future where Mustangs and humans can thrive together, each respecting the other's place in the natural order.

Chapter 4:
Conservation and Advocacy Efforts

"A horse doesn't care how much you know until he knows how much you care."
– Pat Parelli

Picture a small town nestled deep in Mustang country, where the rhythm of life beats in harmony with the distant sound of hooves. In this town, a group of dedicated individuals gathers in a modest community center to strategize about Mustang conservation. Around them are posters of galloping Mustangs and maps of nearby grazing lands—symbols of their shared purpose. These grassroots warriors, armed with passion and perseverance, are part of a growing network of advocates across the nation determined to protect the American Mustang from the threats it faces. This chapter explores the many dimensions of advocacy and conservation, showcasing the triumphs, challenges, and the critical role individuals and communities play in preserving these iconic horses.

Grassroots advocacy forms the backbone of Mustang conservation efforts. These local movements are born from the profound connection people feel toward Mustangs, a connection that inspires action. Small but determined groups organize community events, launch fundraising campaigns, and mobilize public support. Whether hosting workshops about the ecological importance of Mustangs or leading hikes into Mustang habitats to inspire awe and understanding, these grassroots organizations breathe life into conservation efforts.

At the core of these movements are volunteers—ordinary people doing extraordinary work. Volunteers restore degraded habitats, plant native grasses, and maintain watering holes to ensure Mustangs have access to essential resources. Others take on administrative roles, organizing petitions, managing social media pages, or coordinating events. Together, these individuals contribute countless hours to preserve the freedom of Mustangs and raise awareness about their plight.

Social media has amplified the reach of these movements. Platforms like Instagram, Twitter, and Facebook allow advocates to connect with audiences far beyond their local communities. Hashtags such as #SaveTheMustangs and #WildAndFree unite voices into powerful digital campaigns, creating a groundswell of support. Online petitions often gather thousands of signatures within days, demonstrating the widespread public interest in Mustang conservation. These efforts build momentum, showing policymakers that Mustangs have advocates at every level of society.

A sanctuary is defined as a protected area where animals can live freely in their natural habitats or in environments that closely replicate them, without fear of harm or exploitation. Sanctuaries often focus on conservation, rehabilitation, and the humane care of injured, orphaned, or endangered animals. A place where Mustangs roam freely, grazing in peace under an open sky. Mustang sanctuaries just like 3rd Coast Sanctuary offer these horses a second chance, especially those found dumped at auction, injured in the wild, orphaned, or removed from their habitats due to round-ups. Located in regions that closely resemble Mustangs' natural environments, sanctuaries provide a space for these animals to live with minimal human interference.

Daily operations at Mustang sanctuaries involve careful attention to the horses' needs. Caretakers ensure Mustangs receive proper nutrition, monitor their health, and manage herd dynamics. Veterinary teams perform regular checkups, while conservationists work to maintain the habitat. The goal is to create an environment that mirrors the wild as much as possible, allowing Mustangs to thrive without the pressures of urbanization or overpopulation.

Sanctuaries also play a pivotal role in genetic conservation. By managing breeding programs thoughtfully, they help maintain genetic diversity, ensuring the long-term viability of Mustang populations. Healthy genetic diversity is vital for preventing inbreeding, which can lead to weakened herds more susceptible to disease and environmental stressors.

Collaboration enhances the effectiveness of sanctuaries. Partnerships with wildlife organizations, universities, and government agencies bring additional expertise and resources to sanctuary operations. For example, universities may conduct research on grazing patterns or Mustang behavior, contributing valuable data for broader conservation efforts. Educational programs hosted by sanctuaries further their impact by inspiring visitors and involving students in hands-on conservation work.

Despite their importance, Mustang sanctuaries face significant challenges. Funding is a constant concern, as these operations require substantial financial resources to feed and care for the horses, maintain infrastructure, and manage the land. Many sanctuaries rely on donations, grants, and fundraising events to meet their needs. Additionally, balancing public access with the well-being of the horses is a delicate task. While visitor programs raise awareness and generate support, they must be managed carefully to avoid disrupting the Mustangs' natural behaviors.

The fight for Mustangs extends into courtrooms and legislative halls, where legal advocates work tirelessly to uphold protections for these wild horses. Legal advocacy plays a critical role in challenging policies that threaten Mustang populations. Lawsuits are often filed to prevent actions such as destructive round-ups or the sale of Mustangs to slaughterhouses. These legal battles demand accountability from agencies tasked with managing Mustangs and often highlight flaws in current management practices.

One of the most significant pieces of legislation in Mustang conservation is the Wild Free-Roaming Horses and Burros Act of 1971. This law granted Mustangs federal protection and established their place on public lands. However, amendments and policy changes over the years have weakened its impact, leading to continued struggles over land use and population management.

Legal victories, though hard-fought, can have lasting impacts. In recent years, several notable legal cases have involved federal judges intervening in proposed Mustang roundups. These cases have begun to help influence Mustang conservation policies and practices, but sadly so many Mustangs families have been split up as there is no clear-cut legislature to protect them.

In March 2024, U.S. District Court Judge Miranda Du ruled that the Bureau of Land Management (BLM) failed to adopt a legal herd management plan or conduct the necessary environmental review before conducting a roundup in Nevada that resulted in the deaths of 31 Mustangs. Judge Du ordered the BLM to complete a formal herd management plan for the Pancake Complex by March 24, 2025, and to reopen an environmental assessment to include the potential impact of roundups on wildfire risks.

In September 2024, a legal battle concerning the wild horse population in Wyoming was set for the 10th U.S. Circuit Court of Appeals. Mustang advocates challenged a lower court ruling that permitted the BLM to round up and house nearly 5,000 horses in long-term facilities. The BLM was accused of not following due procedures or considering contraception as a population control alternative.

These cases highlight the ongoing legal debates surrounding Mustang management and the role of the judiciary in shaping conservation policies. For example, in a landmark case, a federal judge halted a proposed round-up that would have removed hundreds of Mustangs from their habitat. The decision underscored the importance of adhering to humane management practices and protecting Mustangs' rights to remain on public lands. Such rulings not only safeguard specific herds but also set important precedents that influence future conservation policies.

The Save America's Forgotten Equines (SAFE) Act, designated as H.R.3475 in the House and S.2037 in the Senate, was reintroduced in May 2023 by a bipartisan group of U.S. legislators. This proposed legislation aims to permanently ban horse slaughter within the United States and prohibit the export of horses for slaughter abroad. As of November 2024, the bill remains under consideration in Congress, with advocacy groups urging the public to contact their U.S. senators and representatives to support and cosponsor the SAFE Act, emphasizing the need for swift passage to protect horses from inhumane practices.

Public awareness campaigns often accompany legal efforts, using high-profile cases to draw attention to the plight of Mustangs. Media coverage of court battles can galvanize public support, inspiring more people to engage in advocacy and contribute to conservation efforts.

Amid the challenges, there are also stories of hope and success in Mustang conservation. One notable triumph occurred in Nevada, where a severely threatened herd was brought back from the brink of extinction. Conservationists and local volunteers collaborated to restore the herd's habitat, ensuring access to water and forage. Through these efforts, the herd's numbers stabilized and eventually grew, providing a powerful example of what can be achieved through dedication and teamwork.

Another success story is the establishment of wildlife corridors, which connect fragmented habitats and allow Mustangs to roam freely across larger areas. These corridors not only benefit Mustangs but also support other wildlife, fostering biodiversity and ecosystem health. In some cases, partnerships with private landowners have enabled the expansion of Mustang habitats, creating additional safe spaces for herds to thrive.

Educational programs have also proven effective in fostering public support for Mustangs. Schoolchildren learn about the ecological role and cultural significance of these horses, while hands-on experiences, such as visits to sanctuaries, leave lasting impressions. These programs cultivate a new generation of advocates, ensuring that the fight for Mustangs will continue.

Modern technology has revolutionized Mustang conservation. GPS collars, for instance, provide precise data on Mustang movements, helping researchers understand migration patterns and habitat use. Drones equipped with cameras offer aerial views of herds, allowing conservationists to monitor population sizes and health without intruding on the horses' space.

Satellite imagery and remote sensing technologies also play a vital role in habitat management. By tracking changes in vegetation and water availability, conservationists can identify areas in need of restoration. Artificial intelligence (AI) further enhances these efforts by analyzing data to predict future challenges, enabling proactive conservation strategies.

While these technologies are transformative, they require significant investment and expertise. To maximize their impact, conservation organizations must balance technological tools with traditional methods, ensuring that all approaches complement one another.

The future of Mustang conservation depends not only on large organizations and legal battles but also on the actions of individuals. Becoming a Mustang advocate begins with education—learning about the challenges these horses face and the efforts to protect them. From there, you can choose to volunteer with local advocacy groups, participate in habitat restoration projects, or contribute to fundraising campaigns.

Social media offers an accessible platform for advocacy. Sharing articles, photos, and petitions can amplify the message and inspire others to get involved. Writing to policymakers, attending public meetings, and supporting legislation that benefits Mustangs are also impactful ways to make your voice heard.

By joining the movement to protect Mustangs, you become part of a larger story—a story of resilience, community, and the enduring spirit of the wild. Together, we can ensure that Mustangs continue to roam free, their legacy a testament to the beauty and power of the natural world.

Chapter 5:
A Day in the Life on the Sanctuary

"Horses make a landscape look beautiful."
– Alice Walker

In the heart of my Mustang sanctuary, the day begins as the first light of dawn spills over the horizon, casting a warm glow across the pasture. Fun fact – Mustangs prefer to be out in pasture all day and night, and not inside a barn stall. We found this out after years of stalling them inside, we finally made the leap to let them pasture overnight. After about 6 months we noticed all of their manes and tails had grown about an inch! Here, the routine is both a labor of love and a testament to the dedication of those who choose to devote their lives to these magnificent creatures. The sanctuary buzzes with activity as myself and volunteers work together, each with a specific role that ensures the Mustangs are cared for and their environment is maintained to foster safety and healing. Feeding time is an orchestrated event, as we do bring them inside for breakfast, vet check, grooming and training. After all, they no longer live in the wild, so they have to learn to be handled so they are safe around humans. They then head back to pasture after their time inside, and happily graze, play and nap all day long. Later in the afternoon, they will get supplemental hay bales distributed around the pasture to mimic how they need to eat. It's a delicate balance, ensuring each Mustang receives its fair share, especially when some are still learning to trust humans enough to approach.

The grounds of the sanctuary require constant attention. From mending fences to ensuring that pastures are free of debris, the maintenance of the sanctuary is as crucial as the care of its inhabitants. These tasks, often physically demanding, are undertaken with a sense of purpose, knowing that a well-kept environment contributes significantly to the Mustangs' well-being. The sanctuary must be a place where these horses can roam freely and safely, a refuge from the struggles they have faced elsewhere. Each blade of grass and every stretch of open land serves as a reminder of the sanctuary's mission to provide a second chance for these horses.

The roles within the sanctuary are as varied as they are vital. The team includes veterinarians, a farrier and a few caretakers who help monitor the health of each Mustang, looking for signs of illness or injury. We've all learned to spot the subtle changes in behavior that might indicate a problem, ensuring that any health issues are addressed promptly. Volunteers, often drawn from diverse backgrounds, find themselves learning new skills, from administering basic medical care to engaging with visitors eager to learn about the Mustangs. Their presence is crucial, not just for the labor they provide but for the connection they foster between the sanctuary and the broader community.

Working in a Mustang sanctuary comes with its own set of challenges and rewards. Addressing health issues and emergencies can be emotionally taxing, requiring quick thinking and a calm demeanor. Yet, the rewards of the work are profound. Building connections with individual Mustangs, watching them grow from fearful, uncertain creatures into confident, curious horses, is an experience unlike any other. Each Mustang has a story, and as they settle into sanctuary life, they begin to reveal their personalities. Some are playful, others more reserved, but all are deserving of the care and attention they receive.

Stories from the sanctuary staff and volunteers paint a vivid picture of life in this unique environment. One volunteer recalls the moment a particularly shy, worrried Mustang, named Beni, let her pick up his feet for the first time. It was a moment of trust that took months to build, a small gesture that spoke volumes about the bond they had formed. Another staff member reflects on the impact of their work, noting how each Mustang's journey toward healing mirrors the sanctuary's own evolution. These firsthand accounts capture the essence of sanctuary life, where patience and compassion intersect to create a haven for both horses and humans.

The rescue of a Mustang often begins with an urgent need to remove the horse from a dire situation, whether it's neglect, abuse. Once a Mustang arrives at our sanctuary, the journey from rescue to recovery is both transformative and challenging. Initial assessments are critical. They involve thorough medical evaluations to address any physical ailments the horse may have. Many Mustangs arrive with visible signs of distress, such as malnutrition or injuries, requiring immediate medical intervention to stabilize their health. This phase

is crucial, setting the foundation for the rehabilitation process. With stable health, the focus shifts to the psychological and social rehabilitation of these once-wild creatures.

Behavioral rehabilitation is a nuanced process, requiring time, patience, and a deep understanding of equine psychology. The goal is to help Mustangs transition from survival mode to a state where they can thrive in the presence of humans. Socialization often begins with simple interactions, allowing the Mustang to observe humans from a safe distance. Gradually, we introduce gentle, non-threatening activities like grooming or hand-feeding, fostering a sense of safety and trust. As the Mustang becomes more comfortable, these interactions become more frequent and varied, encouraging the horse to engage with both humans and other horses. This process is vital for Mustangs who have lived in isolation or under stress, as it helps them relearn the social cues that are essential for living in a herd environment.

The stories of Mustangs that have undergone successful rehabilitation are nothing short of inspiring. Take, for example, a Mustang named Mattina, who arrived at our sanctuary as a frightened, unhandled former rodeo bucking horse, with her tiny foal who was born at auction. We spent a full year allowing her to decompress and learn that humans are not all bad. Through dedicated care and attention, Mattina has transformed into a trusting, gentle horse, able to be haltered, led and vet checked, almost eager to interact with both humans and her equine companions. The change in Mattina was not just physical but emotional. She has slowly developed a newfound trust in humans, and every day we see more improvement. Such transformations highlight the resilience of these horses and the profound impact that compassionate care can have on their recovery. They remind us that with the right environment and support, Mustangs can overcome their past traumas and embrace a brighter future.

Despite these successes, the rehabilitation process is fraught with challenges. Many Mustangs arrive with deep-seated trauma and anxiety, making them wary of human interaction. Overcoming these barriers requires a delicate balance of patience and consistency. We must be attuned to each Mustang's individual needs and boundaries, adapting how we approach them as necessary. Integrating Mustangs into existing herds or sanctuary environments poses additional challenges. New arrivals must learn to navigate the social hierarchies of established groups, which can be a source of stress and conflict. Caretakers play an essential role in monitoring these interactions, stepping in when necessary to prevent aggression or bullying.

Rehabilitation efforts are a cornerstone of Mustang conservation, serving both the horses and the broader community. By rehabilitating Mustangs and increasing their adoption rates, sanctuaries help alleviate the pressure on wild populations, reducing the need for drastic population control measures. Moreover, each rehabilitated Mustang serves as a living ambassador for their wild counterparts, educating the public about the challenges these horses face. Through adoption events, educational programs, and public outreach, sanctuaries raise awareness about Mustang welfare, encouraging people to support conservation efforts in any way they can. The journey from rescue to recovery is not just about saving individual horses; it's about preserving the spirit and legacy of the Mustang for generations to come.

Imagine a wide, open field where a Mustang stands beside a human, the two sharing a silent understanding that goes beyond words. The bond that can form between Mustangs and humans is a unique connection filled with depth and meaning, often leading to lifelong partnerships that transform both parties. These bonds begin with simple, everyday interactions, gradually building into profound friendships. As trust grows, a Mustang might nuzzle a familiar hand or follow a human companion, steps that signify acceptance, connection and affection. For the people involved, these relationships often provide a sense of fulfillment and purpose. The companionship of a Mustang can inspire personal growth, teaching lessons of patience, empathy, and resilience. Humans find themselves reflecting on the nature of trust and the power of nonverbal communication, gaining insights that extend beyond the pasture.

The benefits of interacting with Mustangs are not one-sided. These horses, with their gentle presence and intuitive nature, offer therapeutic benefits that have been widely recognized. In equine-assisted therapy programs, Mustangs play a pivotal role in helping individuals cope with emotional and mental challenges. Participants often speak of the calming influence these horses have, providing a sense of peace and grounding. Therapists note that Mustangs, with their ability to mirror human emotions, help clients process feelings and develop coping strategies. The act of caring for a Mustang, whether through grooming or simply being present, can alleviate anxiety and depression, fostering a sense of calm and connection. This therapy is not just about healing; it's about building a bridge between the human and animal worlds, where each learns from the other.

Both Mustangs and humans gain from these connections. For the horses, positive interactions with humans can lead to changes in behavior and demeanor. Mustangs, often wary of human contact, learn to trust and engage, becoming more relaxed and responsive. These interactions enhance their well-being, promoting a sense of security and belonging. Humans, in turn, develop a deeper understanding and empathy for these animals. They learn to read the subtle cues of a Mustang's body language, fostering a relationship built on mutual respect. This enhanced understanding contributes to the broader goals of Mustang conservation, as people become more invested in the welfare of these majestic creatures. The connections formed between Mustangs and humans are not just personal; they resonate with the larger community, promoting a culture of care and stewardship.

Consider the story of a young woman named Lisbeth, who found solace in the company of a paint Mustang gelding named Beni (short for Bendición, meaning blessing). Struggling with personal challenges, Lisbeth was drawn to the quiet strength of these horses. Her time with Beni became a source of healing and inspiration. Each day, she would visit the pasture, where Beni would greet her with a gentle nudge, as if sensing her need for comfort. Through their interactions, Lisbeth discovered a newfound sense of confidence and purpose. Beni, once a skittish and reclusive horse, having been pulled from his wild existence at 15 and still a stallion. Beni blossomed under Lisbeth's care, becoming more trusting. Their bond was more than companionship; it was a testament to the transformative power of understanding and love. Such stories illustrate the profound impact these relationships can have, revealing the possibilities that emerge when humans and Mustangs come together with open hearts. These narratives of connection and transformation are not isolated. They reflect a broader truth about the potential for healing and growth that exists within the human-Mustang relationship. For many, these horses are not just animals; they are partners in a journey of self-discovery and emotional renewal. The lessons learned in the company of Mustangs extend far beyond the pasture, influencing how individuals relate to others and perceive the world around them. Through the simple act of being present with a Mustang, people find themselves changed, awakened to the beauty of the natural world and the power of connection.

Chapter 6:
Visual Storytelling through Photography

"No philosophers so thoroughly comprehend us as dogs and horses."
– Herman Melville

The moment I ventured into the wilds of Wyoming and saw my first truly wild Mustang was transformative—a silhouette framed against a golden horizon, exuding grace and untamed freedom. It was not just a discovery of Mustangs but also my initiation into the world of photography. Leaving behind a career in Hollywood, I was searching for something that resonated with my soul, and in those vast, rugged landscapes, I found it. Photography and Mustangs became intertwined in my journey, each teaching me about the other through education, trial, and error. The patience and precision required to capture these moments paralleled the process of learning about the breed itself—its resilience, social dynamics, and spirit.

I quickly fell in love with Mustangs, their beauty and strength sparking a creative and emotional connection. Natural lighting, especially during the golden hour, became my greatest ally, transforming scenes into breathtaking portraits that highlighted their powerful physiques and expressive eyes. As my passion grew, I began traveling to remote areas to document these magnificent horses in their natural habitats. The rugged landscapes and harsh elements presented challenges, but they only deepened my respect for the Mustangs' ability to adapt and thrive. Through trial, exploration, and countless moments of awe, I found a new purpose—telling their story through the lens, one image at a time, and sharing the spirit of these wild creatures with the world.

Art and photography also play crucial roles in advocacy, influencing public perception and policy. Visual campaigns use compelling imagery to raise awareness, inspire support, and drive conservation efforts. Exhibitions and collaborative projects bring together artists, photographers, and conservationists, amplifying their collective impact. These initiatives engage audiences on emotional and intellectual levels, fostering a deeper appreciation for the Mustangs and the need to protect them.

The power of visual storytelling lies in its ability to evoke emotion and connect people to distant causes. A single image—whether of a Mustang silhouetted against a sunset or a tender moment between mare and foal—can inspire action and advocacy. In a world increasingly driven by visual media, photography and art remain vital tools for preserving the legacy of the Mustang, ensuring that future generations can appreciate the beauty and freedom these wild horses represent.

Chapter 7:
The Future of the American Mustang

"The horse is a mirror to your soul. Sometimes you might not like what you see. Sometimes you will."
— Buck Brannaman

In the vast deserts of the American West, where the horizon stretches endlessly, profound changes are shaping the future of the American Mustang. As the sun casts long shadows over this timeless landscape, the path forward for these iconic horses remains uncertain. These changes—both environmental and human-driven—are defining the challenges and possibilities that will determine the Mustangs' existence for generations to come.

Climate change has become a powerful force altering the Mustangs' habitat. Rising temperatures and diminishing water sources strain their survival, while shifting vegetation patterns reduce forage availability, forcing them to travel farther for sustenance. The arid environments they call home are becoming increasingly inhospitable. Coupled with these challenges is urban development, which fragments traditional roaming grounds with roads, homes, and infrastructure. The spaces where Mustangs once thrived are shrinking, creating conflicts with human populations and other wildlife. Decisions about land use often favor economic development over preservation, leaving Mustangs to navigate an ever-smaller world.

To better understand what lies ahead for Mustangs, scientists use population modeling to predict future trends. These projections paint a stark contrast between potential outcomes. Without intervention, continued habitat loss could lead to sharp declines in Mustang populations, with isolated herds becoming genetically vulnerable. Conversely, strategic conservation efforts could stabilize their numbers, preserving the genetic diversity that ensures their adaptability and resilience. Satellite imagery and data analytics play an essential role in this work, offering real-time insights into habitat changes and population dynamics. These technologies allow conservationists to anticipate challenges and create proactive strategies to safeguard Mustang populations.

Efforts to protect Mustangs require a combination of innovative approaches and targeted action. Protecting key habitats and restoring degraded ecosystems are vital steps in preserving the environments Mustangs depend on. Sustainable grazing practices, such as rotational grazing, can reduce the environmental impact of Mustang populations while maintaining ecosystem balance. Advances in genetic research enable scientists to monitor and preserve genetic diversity, helping prevent the risks of inbreeding within isolated herds. Collaboration among scientists, policymakers, and local communities is crucial in addressing these challenges, ensuring conservation efforts are comprehensive and effective.

Education is a cornerstone of Mustang conservation, inspiring awareness and action. By incorporating Mustang-focused lessons into school curricula, children can develop an appreciation for their ecological and cultural significance, laying the foundation for future advocacy. Public awareness campaigns bring Mustang conservation to broader audiences, using compelling visuals and storytelling to highlight the challenges they face. Documentaries, social media platforms, and other outreach efforts amplify these messages, creating emotional connections that drive support for conservation initiatives.

Community outreach events and workshops further deepen public engagement, offering opportunities for hands-on involvement. Activities like citizen science projects or local art exhibits create meaningful experiences that connect people with Mustangs and their habitats. Partnerships with educational institutions and NGOs extend the reach of these efforts, combining resources and expertise to build networks of advocates. As awareness grows, so does public support for policies and initiatives that prioritize Mustang protection, fostering a cycle of sustained conservation action.

Young people are increasingly stepping into leadership roles in Mustang advocacy, bringing energy and fresh perspectives to the cause. Youth-led groups are organizing events, raising awareness, and actively participating in conservation projects. Whether working on habitat restoration or conducting research on Mustang populations, young advocates are gaining hands-on experience that deepens their commitment to wildlife protection. Mentorship programs and educational expeditions empower these individuals, equipping them with the knowledge and skills to drive meaningful change. By investing in youth engagement, we cultivate the next generation of conservation leaders who will ensure that Mustangs continue to thrive.

Collaboration is critical to Mustang conservation, uniting diverse stakeholders in pursuit of a shared goal. Partnerships between government agencies, non-governmental organizations (NGOs), and local communities bring together resources and expertise, enhancing the impact of conservation efforts. Cross-border initiatives are particularly valuable, as they ensure Mustangs have access to contiguous habitats that support their natural roaming behaviors. Successful collaborative projects demonstrate the power of teamwork, whether through joint research initiatives or coordinated habitat restoration programs. Although differences in priorities among stakeholders can pose challenges, open communication and trust-building are key to overcoming these obstacles.

Recent successes in Mustang conservation offer a sense of hope. Protected habitats have expanded, giving Mustangs the space they need to roam and thrive. Rehabilitation and rewilding programs have rescued Mustangs from captivity and reintegrated them into the wild, bolstering population health and genetic diversity. These achievements have been made possible by innovative conservation strategies, technological advancements, and widespread public support. Stories of resilience and recovery inspire communities, demonstrating that meaningful change is possible when people work together.

Looking to the future, the potential for sustained progress in Mustang conservation is significant. By continuing to invest in research and education, we can build on current successes and address emerging challenges. Expanding proven programs and embracing new technologies will strengthen efforts to protect Mustangs and their habitats. The enduring spirit of these wild horses reminds us of the importance of preserving the untamed beauty of the American landscape. Their survival depends on our collective commitment to conservation, ensuring that future generations can witness Mustangs roaming free across the plains.

Chapter 8:
Mustang Advocacy and Community Engagement

"A horse is worth more than riches."
– Spanish Proverb

Imagine standing on a sunlit hill, the warm breeze carrying the distant sound of Mustangs galloping freely. Your heart stirs with a determination to protect these majestic creatures. This moment, infused with purpose, marks the beginning of a journey into Mustang advocacy. To make a meaningful impact, begin by researching local Mustang advocacy groups. These organizations are the backbone of conservation efforts, working tirelessly to protect Mustangs from various threats. Reach out to them, volunteer at their sanctuaries, attend their meetings, and learn about their ongoing projects. Your involvement can start small, but every step counts. By understanding the landscape of advocacy, you position yourself to contribute effectively.

Individual contributions play a crucial role in the success of collective conservation goals. Volunteering for events and conservation projects allows you to directly impact Mustang welfare. Whether it's helping with habitat restoration, assisting in educational programs, or participating in fundraising events, your efforts contribute to a larger cause. Because of our important supporters, We were able to save over 20 mustangs and donkeys.

Citizen science initiatives offer another way to get involved. These projects often involve collecting data on Mustang populations, behavior, and habitats. By contributing to scientific research, you help build a foundation of knowledge that informs conservation strategies and policy decisions.

There are numerous roles and opportunities within Mustang advocacy, each offering a unique way to contribute. Administrative support is vital for advocacy organizations, ensuring smooth operations and effective communication. If you have skills in organization, communication, or management, consider volunteering your time to help with logistics, event planning, or outreach efforts. Educational outreach is another impactful avenue. By engaging with schools and communities, you can raise awareness about Mustangs and inspire others to join the cause. These efforts are essential in building a culture of conservation, where the next generation is informed and motivated to protect these iconic horses.

Getting involved in advocacy can seem daunting, especially when faced with common barriers like time constraints and geographical limitations. However, with careful planning, these challenges can be overcome. Effective time management is key. Set aside dedicated time each week to focus on advocacy activities, whether it's attending meetings, volunteering, or engaging in educational efforts.

Virtual participation offers a solution to geographical limitations. Many organizations host webinars, online workshops, and virtual meetings, allowing you to contribute from anywhere. This flexibility ensures that distance is not a barrier to making a difference.

Reflecting on my journey into Mustang advocacy, I never imagined starting a Mustang sanctuary with so little experience. Yet, fueled by passion and a desire to make a difference, I took the leap. I began with the support of a dedicated group of followers who shared my vision, their encouragement and belief in the cause bolstering my confidence. Together, we built something meaningful, step by step. With no formal background but an eagerness to learn, I sought guidance from seasoned advocates, dove into research, and leaned on the expertise of those who had walked this path before. Each challenge became an opportunity to grow, and each small success strengthened our resolve. As I found my place in this vibrant community, the sanctuary became more than just a safe haven for Mustangs—it became a symbol of what passion and collective effort can achieve.

Creating a strong network in Mustang advocacy is like weaving a safety net, each thread connecting individuals and organizations working towards a shared goal. These connections allow access to a wealth of shared resources and knowledge, fostering an environment where ideas can flow freely. When you are part of a robust network, you gain visibility and influence, amplifying the reach of your conservation campaigns. This collective strength can open doors to funding opportunities, collaborative projects, and increased public awareness. Imagine the impact of pooling expertise from various fields—scientists, policymakers, and passionate volunteers—each bringing their own perspective and skills to the table. Together, these groups can push for meaningful change and innovative solutions to the challenges Mustangs face.

Networking begins with stepping out and meeting others who share your passion. Attending conferences and networking events is a powerful way to start. These gatherings provide a platform to connect with like-minded individuals, each with their own stories and experiences to share. Conversations at these events can spark new ideas and collaborations that might not have been possible otherwise. Online platforms also play a vital role in building connections. Social media groups, forums, and professional networks offer spaces where advocates can discuss strategies, share updates, and support one another. By engaging with these communities, you can stay informed about the latest advocacy efforts and learn from the successes and challenges faced by others in the field.

Collaboration is the heartbeat of successful advocacy. By joining forces with other environmental groups, you can amplify your impact. These partnerships can lead to joint initiatives that address broader environmental issues while keeping Mustang conservation at the forefront. Cross-sector collaborations with businesses and government agencies can also be highly effective. Such partnerships can provide access to additional resources and influence, creating a united front capable of driving policy changes and increasing public engagement. When diverse groups work together, they bring a range of perspectives and expertise, allowing for more comprehensive approaches to conservation challenges.

There are inspiring examples of advocacy networks that have achieved significant outcomes. Regional Mustang alliances, for instance, bring together local stakeholders to focus on issues specific to their areas. These coalitions often include ranchers, conservationists, and government officials working side by side, demonstrating the power of collaboration. Global partnerships focused on wild horse conservation have also made strides, uniting organizations across countries to share research, strategies, and resources. These networks highlight the potential of collective action to create lasting change, showing that when people come together, they can accomplish what might seem impossible alone.

Effective social media advocacy hinges on creating content that captures attention and inspires sharing. The visual appeal is crucial; striking images or videos showcasing the beauty and plight of Mustangs can captivate audiences, prompting them to learn more and get involved. Crafting shareable content means considering what resonates with your audience—whether it's awe-inspiring photos of wild Mustangs or infographics that simplify complex issues. Utilizing hashtags strategically can also amplify your message, increasing its visibility in crowded digital spaces. Hashtags that are memorable and relevant allow users to discover related content and join broader conversations, creating a ripple effect that extends the reach of your advocacy efforts.

Successful social media campaigns demonstrate the power of digital platforms to effect change. One example involves a viral campaign that used powerful storytelling and visuals to raise significant funds for Mustang conservation. By partnering with influencers who share a passion for wildlife, the campaign reached audiences far beyond the immediate conservation community. These influencers, with their large followings, lend credibility and amplify messages, reaching new demographics and encouraging diverse groups to join the cause. Such partnerships are invaluable, as they can transform a campaign from a small-scale effort into a widespread movement, bringing attention to issues that might otherwise remain under the radar.

However, navigating social media advocacy comes with its set of challenges. Balancing authenticity with strategic messaging is critical; while it's important to maintain a genuine voice, the content must also align with overarching advocacy goals. Authenticity fosters trust

and connection with audiences, encouraging them to engage more deeply. Yet, strategic planning ensures that each post or update contributes to a cohesive narrative, one that steadily builds support for conservation efforts. Another challenge lies in managing criticism and misinformation, which can spread quickly on these platforms. Addressing negative comments with factual information and a respectful tone is essential, as is correcting misinformation promptly to maintain credibility. Engaging with users thoughtfully can turn detractors into supporters, demonstrating the power of constructive dialogue in advocacy.

Conclusion

As we close this journey, it's vital to reflect on the profound importance of Mustangs in America. These majestic creatures are more than just symbols of the wild; they embody the spirit of freedom and resilience. From their introduction to the Americas by Spanish explorers to their integral role in shaping indigenous cultures and aiding settlers in westward expansion, Mustangs have been pivotal. They have served in military campaigns and inspired countless myths of the American frontier. Their legacy is woven into the very fabric of American history, culture, and ecology.

Today, however, Mustangs face unprecedented challenges. Urban sprawl encroaches on their habitats, legal battles over land and population control persist, and overpopulation poses ecological threats. Yet, amid these challenges, diverse conservation efforts offer hope. Grassroots movements rally communities, sanctuaries provide safe havens, and technological innovations enhance monitoring and management. Legal advocacy works tirelessly to shape policies that protect these iconic animals. These strategies collectively strive to ensure that Mustangs continue to thrive in the landscapes they have long called home.

Throughout this book, personal stories have underscored the emotional connections between humans and Mustangs. Such narratives reveal the transformative power of these relationships, showcasing healing, advocacy, and inspiration. People from all walks of life have found solace, strength, and purpose through their interactions with Mustangs. These stories remind us of the deep bonds that can form between species, encouraging empathy and understanding.

Visual storytelling has played a crucial role in capturing the essence of Mustangs. Through photography and art, these creatures' grace and power are brought to life, shaping public perception and fostering emotional engagement. The images and artistic expressions serve

as potent tools for advocacy, turning abstract concepts into tangible realities that resonate with the public. They inspire action, drawing attention to the urgent need for conservation.

Looking forward, the future of Mustang conservation holds promise. Innovative strategies such as genetic technologies and eco-friendly grazing practices offer new pathways for protection. Education and youth engagement are equally vital, nurturing a generation that values and advocates for Mustangs. Collaborative efforts, both local and global, are essential in building a united front that addresses the multifaceted challenges these horses face. By working together, we can ensure a thriving future for Mustangs, where they continue to roam free and inspire generations to come.

I invite you to take an active role in Mustang conservation. Join local advocacy groups, support sanctuaries, and spread awareness through storytelling and social media. Your voice and actions can make a significant difference. Share your passion with others, engage in community events, and contribute to the collective effort to protect these magnificent creatures. Every small step contributes to a larger movement, fostering a sense of community and shared purpose.

As we conclude, remember that optimism and hope are powerful drivers of change. Recent successes in Mustang conservation demonstrate the impact of collective action and inspire us to continue this important work. Let us maintain our commitment to Mustang protection and advocacy, ensuring that these wild symbols of freedom remain a vibrant part of our world.

Reflect on this journey and consider your role in the ongoing story of Mustang conservation. What will you do to ensure their legacy endures? As the sun sets on this chapter, let it rise on a future where Mustangs continue to thrive, reminding us of the beauty and resilience of the wild

About the Author

Jennifer Glassman is a passionate advocate for the preservation of wild Mustangs, horses, and donkeys, whose writing and photography not only highlight their beauty but also brings awareness to the inhumane treatment many of these animals face. Through her photography and her nonprofit organization, @3rdcoastsanctuary, Glassman aims to protect these sentient beings from brutal practices such as illegal roundups, poor treatment in Government holding facilities, and the heart-wrenching reality of being shipped across international borders for slaughter.

All proceeds from her photography and books goes to support the herd of rescues @3rdcoastsanctuary, which offers a safe haven for Mustangs, horses, and donkeys that have been rescued from life-threatening situations. This sanctuary focuses on rehabilitating animals that have faced abuse or neglect and works to prevent their tragic fate in the illegal horse meat trade—a practice that involves shipping horses to foreign countries for slaughter. This issue is particularly urgent as tens of thousands of American horses are shipped each year to places like Canada and Mexico, where animal welfare standards can be far less regulated.

With her writing and Mustang-focused photography, Glassman seeks to raise awareness about this crisis and galvanize public support for protecting these animals. She joins a growing movement that calls for the end of such practices and for stronger legislation to protect American horses from being exploited for slaughter. Through her imagery, nonprofit work, and advocacy, Glassman strives to ensure that future generations will be able to witness these majestic creatures thriving in the wild, free from the threat of inhumane treatment.

Glassman's career spans over 25 years in entertainment industry marketing, publicity, and event production, where she has led campaigns for both commercial and charitable causes. Since 2010, she has focused on Mustang Advocacy through her fine art photography, hands-on sanctuary care of her rescued herd, and writing. Glassman lives with her husband in Metamora, Michigan, with their 28 rescued Mustangs, Horses, Donkeys, Dogs and Cats.

All Proceeds from the sales of Glassman's work go to support
horses and donkeys in need and the rescue herd @3rdcoastsanctuary.

References

Hernán Cortés: Conqueror of the Aztecs https://www.livescience.com/39238-hernan-cortes-conqueror-of-the-aztecs.html

THE HISTORY - America's Mustang Story https://www.americasmustang.com/the-history

The Shared History of Wild Horses and Indigenous People https://www.yesmagazine.org/environment/2020/04/27/native-horses-indigenous-history

The History of the Mustang Horse Breed: From Wild to Iconic https://creaturescorner.com/horses/the-history-of-the-mustang-horse-breed-from-wild-to-iconic/

How the Mustang, the Symbol of the Frontier, Became a ... https://www.smithsonianmag.com/history/mustang-symbol-frontier-became-nuisance-180962771/

Wild mustangs and the working cowboys of ... https://www.piquenewsmagazine.com/travel/wild-mustangs-and-the-working-cowboys-of-wyoming-2498676

Mustangs in the U.S. Army https://www.blm.gov/blog/2021-12-02/mustangs-us-army

Mustang: The Saga of the Wild Horse in the American West http://www.deannestillman.com/mustang.shtml

Wild Horses and the Ecosystem https://americanwildhorse.org/wild-horses-and-ecosystem

Wild and Free-Roaming Horses and Burros Act of 1971 https://en.wikipedia.org/wiki/Wild_and_Free-Roaming_Horses_and_Burros_Act_of_1971

What's to Be Done About the Wild Horse Herds of ... https://www.sierraclub.org/sierra/2023-2-summer/feature/what-s-be-done-about-wild-horse-herds-american-west

BLM investing in healthy wild horse herds and wildlife ... https://www.blm.gov/blog/2023-02-06/blm-investing-healthy-wild-horse-herds-and-wildlife-habitat-sand-wash-basin

Advocacy | American Wild Horse Campaign https://americanwildhorse.org/advocacy

Preserving the Majesty of the American Mustang https://mustangvalleysanctuary.com/american-mustang/

Wild Horse Advocates Win lawsuit challenging Bureau of ... https://www.speciesunite.com/news-stories/wild-horse-advocates-win-lawsuit-challenging-bureau-of-land-managements-handling-ofmustang-roundups

Ford Mach-E Research | Features, Trims, Technology & FAQ https://www.autonationfordwestlake.com/research/ford-mustang-mach-e.htm

Meet the mustang whisperer of Windhorse Ranch https://www.pressdemocrat.com/article/news/meet-the-mustang-whisperer-of-windhorse-ranch/

Mustang Rescue Companion | Volunteer in the United ... https://www.volunteerworld.com/en/volunteer-program/mustang-rescue-companion-in-united-states-of-america-mims-florida

Evanescent Mustang Rescue and Sanctuary - Mustang, Rescue https://evanescentmustangrescue.org/

How mustangs help Veterans - VA News https://news.va.gov/80463/mustangs-help-veterans/

Wild Horse Fine Art Photographer Kimerlee Curyl https://www.kimerleecuryl.com/

Wild Horse Art & The History of Mustangs In Paso Robles https://www.mariamarriott.com/post/wild-horse-art-and-the-history-of-mustangs-in-paso-robles

The impact of conservation photography https://blog.adobe.com/en/publish/2021/10/19/conservation-photography-photojournalism-using-your-photography-environmental-conservation

The Art of Saving Wild Horses https://wildmustangsforever.com/the-art-of-saving-wild-horses/

2023 Wild Horse and Burro Population Estimates https://www.blm.gov/sites/default/files/docs/2023-04/2023_HMA-HA_PopStats_4-3-2023_Final.pdf

The Future of America's Wild Horses: The Options https://www.nationalgeographic.com/adventure/article/wild-horse-management-options

The Nature Conservancy's Youth Engagement Programs https://www.nature.org/en-us/about-us/who-we-are/how-we-work/youth-engagement/

Collaborative Conservation | U.S. Fish & Wildlife Service https://www.fws.gov/stakeholder-engagement/resource/collaborative-conservation

Advocacy | American Wild Horse Campaign https://americanwildhorse.org/advocacy

Wild Mustang/Burro Campaigns https://www.luckythreeranch.com/wild-mustang-burro-campaigns/

Tactics In Practice: The Science Of Social Media Advocacy https://faunalytics.org/tactics-in-practice-the-science-of-social-media-advocacy/

Organize Your Own Event https://www.wilderness.org/get-involved/join-our-movement/organize-your-own-event

Download 20 fun facts about
Mustangs and Horses Here!

www.ingramcontent.com/pod-product-compliance
Lightning Source LLC
Chambersburg PA
CBRC102257090526
44582CB00016B/196